ENVIRONMENT
Infographics

Chris Oxlade

Chicago, Illinois

To contact Capstone Global Library, please
call 800-747-4992, or visit our web site
www.capstonepub.com

Edited by Rebecca Rissman, Dan Nunn, and
   John-Paul Wilkins
Designed by Philippa Jenkins
Original illustrations © Capstone Global Library Ltd 2014
Illustrations by HL Studios
Picture research by Elizabeth Alexander
Production by Vicki Fitzgerald
Originated by Capstone Global Library Ltd
Printed and bound in China

17 16 15 14 13
10 9 8 7 6 5 4 3 2 1

Library of Congress Cataloging-in-Publication Data
Oxlade, Chris.
   Environment / Chris Oxlade.
      pages cm.—(Infographics)
   Includes bibliographical references and index.
   ISBN 978-1-4109-6217-1 (hardback)—ISBN 978-1-4109-
6222-5 (paperback) 1. Graphic methods—Juvenile literature. 2.
Charts, diagrams, etc.—Juvenile literature. 3. Ecology—Juvenile
literature. 4. Environmental protection—Juvenile literature. I. Title.
   QA90.O955 2014
   304.2072'8—dc23   2013012530

Acknowledgments
We would like to thank the following for permission to reproduce
photographs: Capstone Global Library p. 4; Shutterstock pp.
4 (© M.Stasy, © Pakhnyushcha, © Stella Caraman, © Thomas
Bethge), 28 (© Complot).

We would like to thank Diana Bentley and Marla Conn for their
invaluable help in the preparation of this book.

Every effort has been made to contact copyright holders
of any material reproduced in this book. Any omissions
will be rectified in subsequent printings if notice is given to
the publisher.

Metric Conversions

Distance and Area
1 meter = 3.3 feet
1 kilometer = 0.6 mile
1 square kilometer = 0.4 square mile

Weight
1 kilogram = 2.2 pounds
1 metric ton = 1.1 tons

Volume
1 gallon = 4.5 liters
100 cubic feet = 2.8 cubic meters

CONTENTS

Some words are shown in bold, **like this**. You can find out what they mean by looking in the glossary.

ABOUT INFOGRAPHICS

An infographic is a picture that gives you information. Infographics can be graphs, charts, maps, or other sorts of pictures. The infographics in this book are about the environment.

Infographics make information easier to understand. We see infographics all over the place, every day. They appear in books, newspapers, on television, on web sites, on posters, and in advertisements.

How much water we use

Here is a simple infographic. It shows how much water one family uses each day.

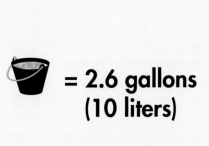 = 2.6 gallons (10 liters)

Average U.S. household

WATER

What do we use water for?

This infographic shows how we use water for different things.

This number is a percentage. It means 27 gallons out of every 100 gallons.

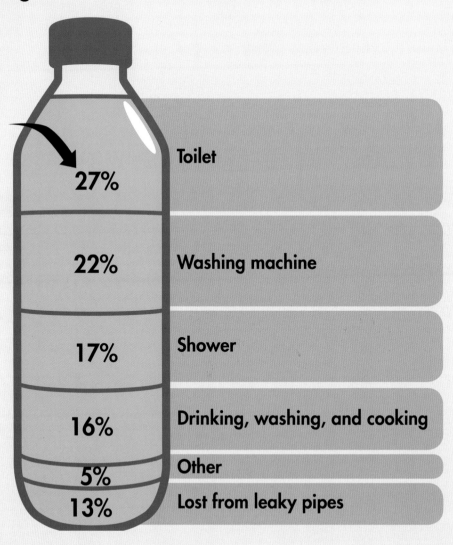

27% Toilet

22% Washing machine

17% Shower

16% Drinking, washing, and cooking

5% Other

13% Lost from leaky pipes

How much water?

This infographic shows how much water different activities use up at home.

 flushing the toilet
3 gallons

 taking a shower
2 gallons a minute

 washing machine
26 gallons

 running a faucet
1 gallon a minute

 filling a bath
2 gallons a minute

 dishwasher load
11 gallons

Farms and factories need much more water than homes. This graph shows how much water is used in farming and industry, compared with at home.

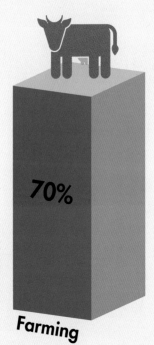

70%

20%

10%

Homes

Industry

Farming

Water use around the world?

People in different countries use different amounts of water. Some use lots, while some use only a little. This map shows how much water a person uses every day in different places.

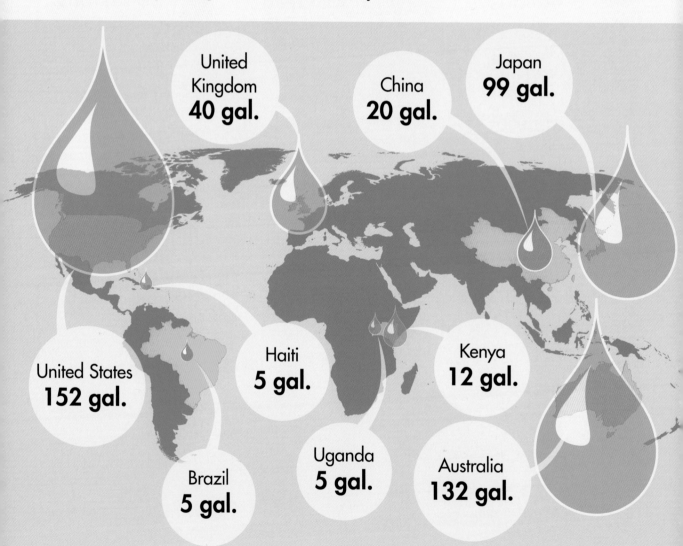

United Kingdom
40 gal.

China
20 gal.

Japan
99 gal.

United States
152 gal.

Haiti
5 gal.

Kenya
12 gal.

Brazil
5 gal.

Uganda
5 gal.

Australia
132 gal.

Saving water

Water is precious. In some parts of the world, there is not enough to go around. Using less water is also good for the environment. This chart shows some ways to save water, and how much water they save.

 Put a plastic bottle of water in the toilet cistern **¼ gallon** per flush

Take a shower instead of a bath Up to **11 gallons**

 Fix a leaky faucet Up to **5 gallons** a day

 Turn off the faucet when you brush your teeth **2 gallons**

 Sponge wash the car instead of hosing Up to **40 gallons**

Bath or shower?

This chart shows how much water you use by taking a shower instead of taking a bath.

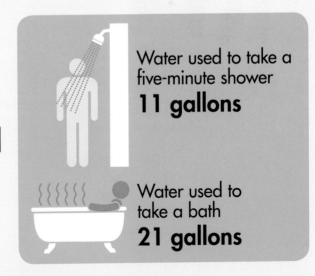

Water used to take a five-minute shower **11 gallons**

Water used to take a bath **21 gallons**

WASTE

Every day we throw away waste, such as food packaging and empty cans. This infographic shows how much waste people in the United States make.

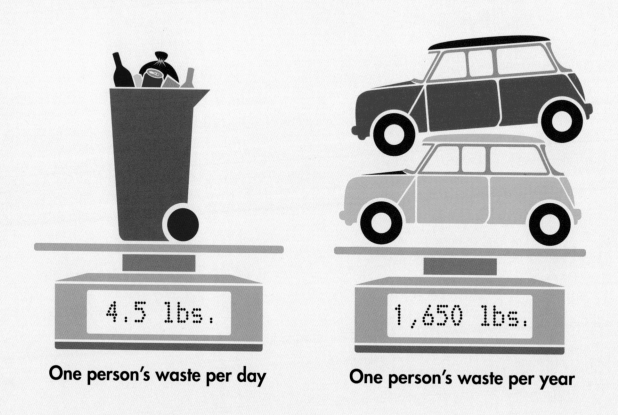

One person's waste per day

4.5 lbs.

One person's waste per year

1,650 lbs.

What sort of waste?

This pie chart shows how much of each sort of waste people in the United States throw away each year.

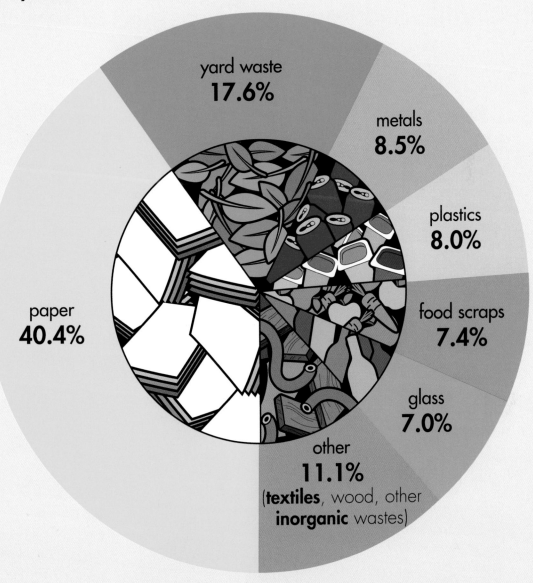

yard waste
17.6%

metals
8.5%

plastics
8.0%

paper
40.4%

food scraps
7.4%

glass
7.0%

other
11.1%
(**textiles**, wood, other **inorganic** wastes)

Waste in the ground

In many countries, most waste is buried in the ground. This is called a **landfill**. This infographic shows how much of the United States' waste goes into landfill, and how much is burned or **recycled**.

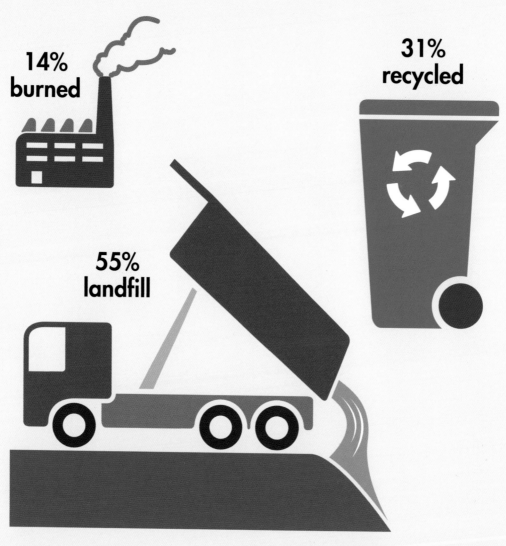

14% burned

31% recycled

55% landfill

Rotting away

Waste that we put in the ground slowly rots away. This infographic shows how long different sorts of waste takes to rot away.

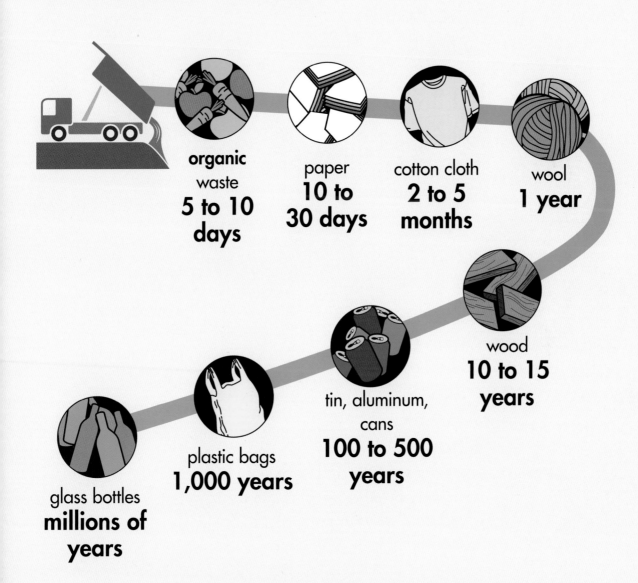

organic waste
5 to 10 days

paper
10 to 30 days

cotton cloth
2 to 5 months

wool
1 year

wood
10 to 15 years

tin, aluminum, cans
100 to 500 years

plastic bags
1,000 years

glass bottles
millions of years

RECYCLING

Plastic bottle recycling facts

This infographic shows some facts about recycling plastic bottles.

1 in 4

The number of plastic bottles that are recycled in the United Kingdom

36 billion

The number of plastic water bottles sold in the United States each year

20

The number of large plastic bottles needed to make a recycled backpack

2.5 million

The number of plastic bottles thrown away in the United States every hour

6 hours

The length of time a 60-watt light bulb could be powered by using the energy saved from recycling one plastic bottle instead of making a new one

Aluminum recycling facts

Here are some facts about recycling aluminum drinking cans.

6,000
New aluminum drinking cans made in the United States every second

60 days
The time between throwing an aluminum can away and its aluminum getting back on the shelves of a store in another can

3 hours
The length of time a television can be powered by using the energy saved from recycling one aluminum can instead of making a new one

56 billion
The number of aluminum cans recycled in the United States every year

Paper recycling facts

Here are some facts about recycling paper.

24
The number of trees that have to be cut down to make 1 ton of newspapers

71 million tons
The total weight of paper and cardboard used in the United States each year

334 pounds
The average weight of paper recycled by each person in the United States each year

7,000 gallons
The amount of water saved by recycling a ton of paper

What do we recycle?

This chart shows the amount of different materials that are recycled each year.

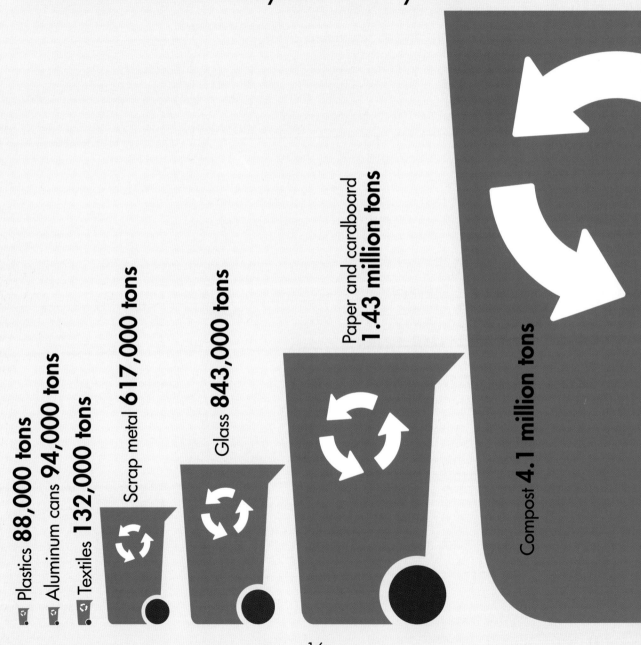

Plastics **88,000 tons**

Aluminum cans **94,000 tons**

Textiles **132,000 tons**

Scrap metal **617,000 tons**

Glass **843,000 tons**

Paper and cardboard **1.43 million tons**

Compost **4.1 million tons**

The best recyclers

This map shows how much waste different countries recycle.

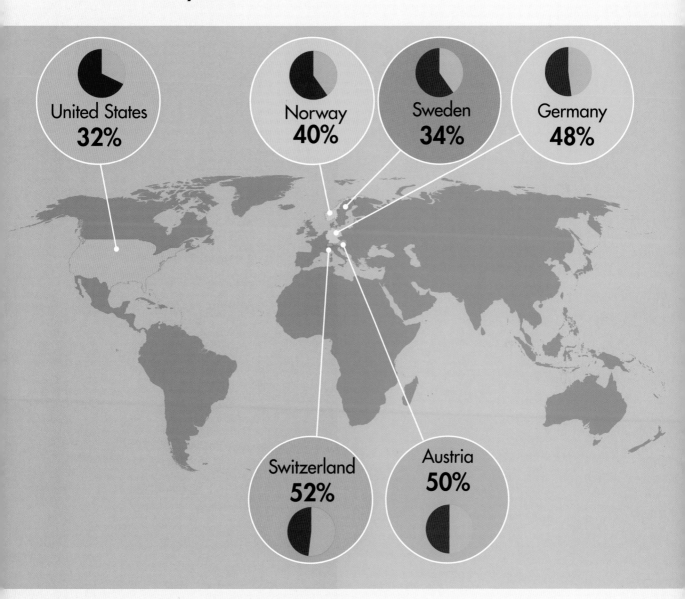

United States
32%

Norway
40%

Sweden
34%

Germany
48%

Switzerland
52%

Austria
50%

POLLUTION

Pollution is waste that goes into rivers, lakes, and the sea, into the air, and onto the land. Pollution is bad for the environment because it harms plants and animals and the places where they live.

Plastic bags are one of the worst sorts of pollution. Here are some facts about plastic-bag pollution.

1.2 trillion
The number of plastic bags used every year in the world

1 million
The number of seabirds killed each year by eating plastic bags and other plastics

12 minutes
The average time that a plastic bag is used for

6 in 100
The number of plastic bags that are recycled in Europe

1,200
The number of plastic bags used by each person in the United States every year

1,000 years
The **estimated** time it takes for a plastic bag to rot away

Trash on the beach

Lots of waste is washed up on beaches. This infographic shows how many pieces of different waste were found on beaches in San Diego County, California, in one year.

55,100
cigarettes and butts

5,800
plastic lids, cups, and straws

10,150
pieces of paper

4,350
pieces of glass

5,800
plastic bottle caps

14,500
bits of **Styrofoam**

15,950
other plastic things

2,900
plastic bags

10,150
plastic food wrappers

20,300
other things

The biggest oil spills

Oil is pumped from under the sea by oil rigs and is carried around the world in huge tankers. Sometimes there are accidents, and oil gets into the sea and onto beaches. This map shows some of the worst oil spills.

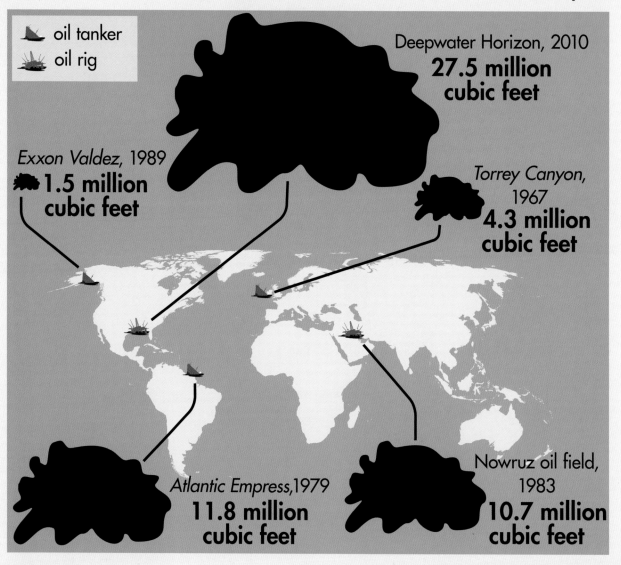

oil tanker
oil rig

Exxon Valdez, 1989
1.5 million cubic feet

Deepwater Horizon, 2010
27.5 million cubic feet

Torrey Canyon, 1967
4.3 million cubic feet

Atlantic Empress,1979
11.8 million cubic feet

Nowruz oil field, 1983
10.7 million cubic feet

Noise pollution

Noise is not the sort of waste you can see or touch. But very loud noise spoils our environment because it is unpleasant and annoying. This infographic shows how loud different noises are.

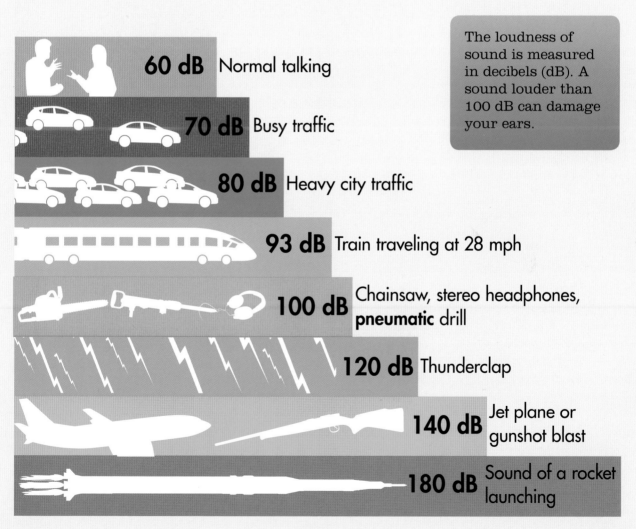

The loudness of sound is measured in decibels (dB). A sound louder than 100 dB can damage your ears.

60 dB Normal talking

70 dB Busy traffic

80 dB Heavy city traffic

93 dB Train traveling at 28 mph

100 dB Chainsaw, stereo headphones, **pneumatic** drill

120 dB Thunderclap

140 dB Jet plane or gunshot blast

180 dB Sound of a rocket launching

ENERGY

We need energy to heat our homes, to make machines and gadgets work, and to travel in cars, trains, and planes. Most of the energy we use comes from oil, coal, and gas. This chart shows the things energy is used for in homes.

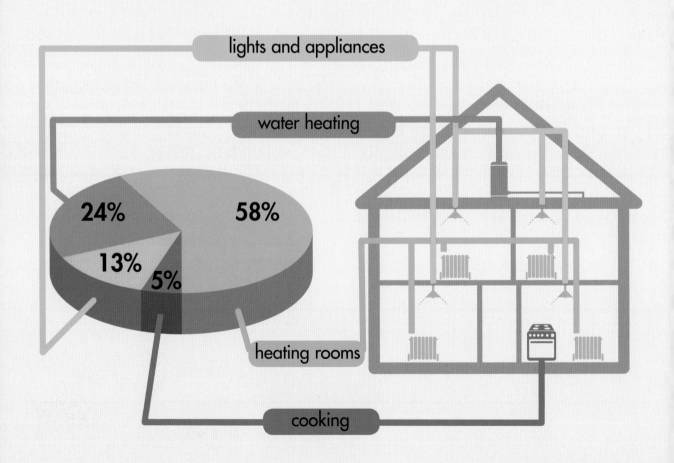

lights and appliances

water heating

24%

58%

13%

5%

heating rooms

cooking

How much electricity we use

This infographic shows how much electricity each person uses every day at home in the United States.

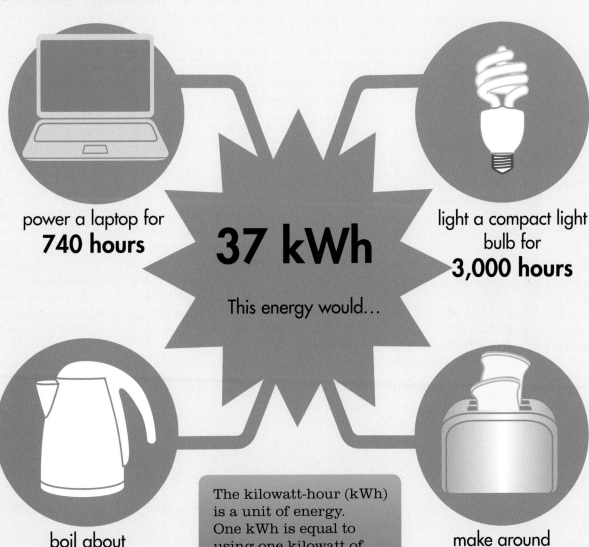

power a laptop for
740 hours

light a compact light bulb for
3,000 hours

37 kWh

This energy would...

boil about
86 gallons
of water in a kettle

The kilowatt-hour (kWh) is a unit of energy. One kWh is equal to using one kilowatt of energy for one hour.

make around
2,000 pieces
of toast

Where energy comes from

This bar chart shows where the world's energy comes from. Most energy comes from oil, coal, and gas. These are called fossil fuels. Renewable energy includes solar energy and wind energy.

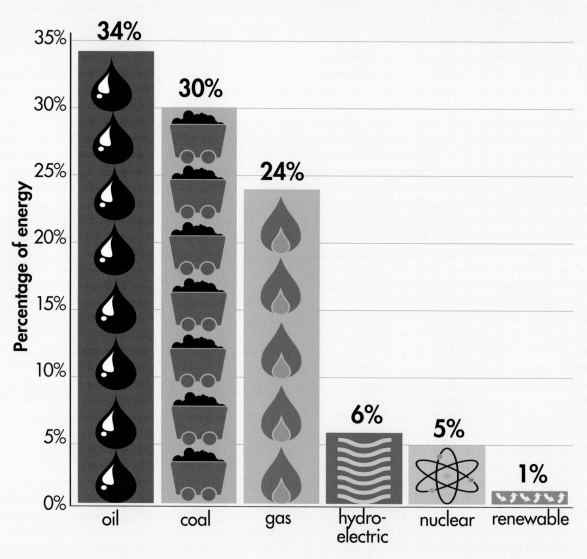

The need for energy

This bar chart shows how the world needs more and more energy each year. It is predicted that energy use will more than double between 1990 and 2035. This is because countries such as China and India are growing fast.

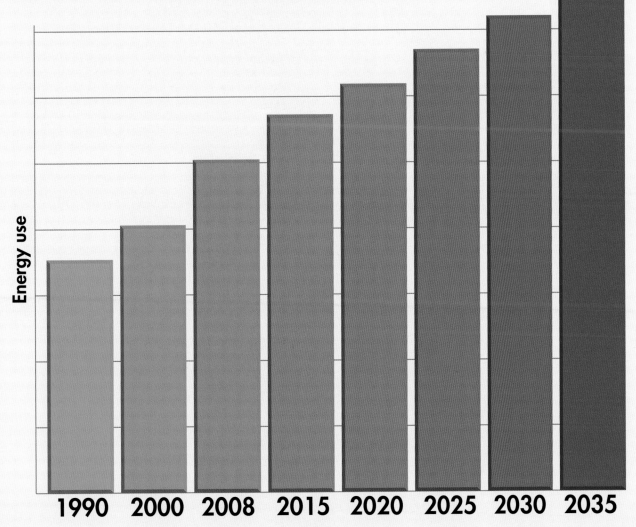

SAVING ENERGY

Using energy is bad for the environment. This is because burning fuels makes pollution in the air. If we use less energy, we help the environment. We also spend less money on electricity!

This chart shows different ways to save energy and how much energy they save.

Only boil as much water as you need. The amount of energy it takes to boil 4 cups of water could power a refrigerator for **7 hours**.

Don't leave lights switched on. A 60-watt light bulb left on for one week costs about the same as **2 chocolate bars**.

Cycling 6 miles instead of driving saves about **¼ gallon** of fuel.

Insulating the attic of a house could save enough energy each day to make around **400 cups** of tea.

Light bulb energy

This chart shows the amount of energy needed to light different sorts of light bulbs. Bulbs that use less energy are better for the environment.

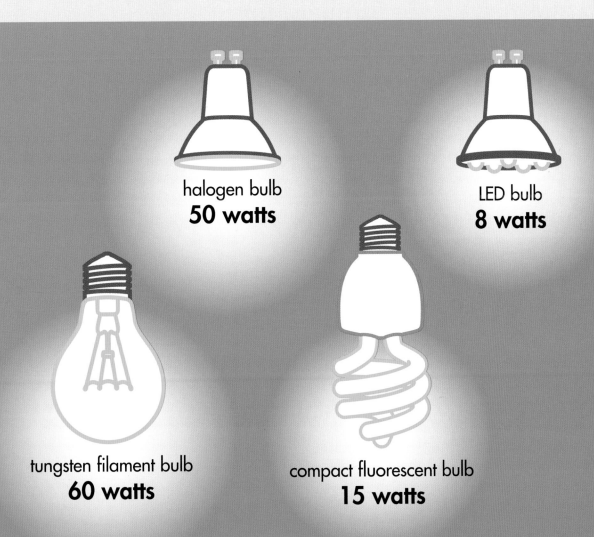

halogen bulb
50 watts

LED bulb
8 watts

tungsten filament bulb
60 watts

compact fluorescent bulb
15 watts

NATURE IN DANGER

Losing the rain forest

The world's rain forests are being chopped down to make space for farming, for mining, and to get wood. This infographic shows how much forest is being chopped down.

50,000 square miles of rain forest are lost a year. That is an area the size of Louisiana.

That is the same as
36 soccer fields per minute

Melting ice

Each year, there is less frozen ocean at the North Pole, where animals such as polar bears live. This means polar animals are losing their **habitat**.

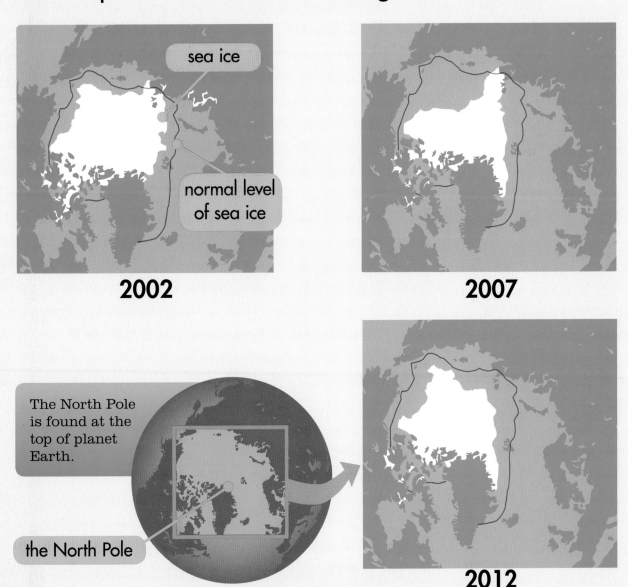

sea ice

normal level of sea ice

2002

2007

The North Pole is found at the top of planet Earth.

the North Pole

2012

GLOSSARY

estimate make a guess about the amount, size, or value of something

habitat place where a plant or animal lives

inorganic not made from plants or animals

landfill waste that is buried in the ground

organic made from plants or animals

pneumatic powered using air

pollution materials that damage the environment, such as plastic and gases from cars

recycle use the materials in an object to make new objects

Styrofoam type of plastic used to make cups, food trays, and packaging

textile cloth or fabric

trillion number that is equal to one thousand times one billion; 1,000,000,000,000

FIND OUT MORE

Books

Bodach, Vijaya. Making Graphs (series). Mankato, Minn.: Capstone, 2008.

Green, Jen. *Why Should I Save Water?* (Why Should I?). Hauppauge, N.Y.: Barron's Educational Series, 2005.

Oxlade, Chris. *Garbage and Recycling* (How Does My Home Work?). Chicago: Heinemann Library, 2013.

Web sites

Facthound offers a safe, fun way to find web sites related to this book. All the sites on Facthound have been researched by our staff.
Here's all you do:
Visit www.facthound.com
Type in this code: 9781410962171

INDEX